50 Kitchen Adventures Recipes

By: Kelly Johnson

Table of Contents

- Sushi Rolls
- Homemade Pasta
- Paella
- Dim Sum
- Ramen from Scratch
- Beef Wellington
- Dumplings
- Thai Green Curry
- Moussaka
- Croissants
- Chicken Shawarma
- Korean BBQ
- Tagine
- Homemade Tortillas
- Sushi Burritos
- Empanadas
- Risotto
- Pho
- Tacos al Pastor
- Jambalaya
- Tamales
- Kimchi
- Gnocchi
- Banh Mi
- Burrata with Roasted Veggies
- Paella Valenciana
- Ceviche
- Chicken Kiev
- Coq au Vin
- Shakshuka
- Peking Duck
- Beef and Ale Pie
- Ravioli from Scratch
- French Onion Soup
- Samosas

- Tarte Tatin
- Risotto alla Milanese
- Croque Monsieur
- Sautéed Frog Legs
- Ratatouille
- Mussels in White Wine Sauce
- Szechuan Stir-fry
- Frittata
- Bouillabaisse
- Bangers and Mash
- Arancini
- Croissant Sandwiches
- Korma Curry
- Goulash
- Pork Schnitzel

Sushi Rolls

Ingredients:

- 2 cups sushi rice
- 2 1/2 cups water
- 1/4 cup rice vinegar
- 2 tablespoons sugar
- 1 teaspoon salt
- 10 sheets nori (seaweed)
- 1 cucumber, julienned
- 1 avocado, sliced
- 1/2 pound sushi-grade tuna or salmon, thinly sliced
- Soy sauce (for dipping)
- Pickled ginger (optional)
- Wasabi (optional)

Instructions:

1. Rinse the sushi rice in cold water until the water runs clear. Combine the rice and water in a pot and bring to a boil. Reduce the heat to low, cover, and simmer for 18 minutes. Remove from heat and let sit, covered, for 10 minutes.
2. While the rice is cooling, mix the rice vinegar, sugar, and salt in a small bowl until dissolved.
3. Gently fold the vinegar mixture into the rice and allow the rice to cool to room temperature.
4. Place a sheet of nori on a bamboo sushi mat with the shiny side facing down.
5. With wet fingers, spread a thin layer of rice over the nori, leaving a 1-inch border at the top.
6. Add cucumber, avocado, and fish in a line across the center of the rice.
7. Carefully roll the sushi using the bamboo mat, starting from the bottom and rolling tightly.
8. Use a sharp knife to slice the roll into bite-sized pieces.
9. Serve with soy sauce, pickled ginger, and wasabi.

Homemade Pasta

Ingredients:

- 2 cups all-purpose flour (plus extra for dusting)
- 2 large eggs
- 1/2 teaspoon salt
- Water (if needed)

Instructions:

1. On a clean surface, make a mound with the flour and create a well in the center.
2. Crack the eggs into the well and add the salt. Use a fork to gently beat the eggs and gradually mix in the flour.
3. Once the dough begins to come together, knead with your hands until smooth and elastic (about 10 minutes). If the dough is too dry, add a teaspoon of water at a time until it reaches the right consistency.
4. Wrap the dough in plastic wrap and let it rest for 30 minutes at room temperature.
5. After resting, roll out the dough using a pasta machine or a rolling pin until it's thin (about 1/16 inch thick).
6. Cut the dough into your desired shape (fettuccine, tagliatelle, etc.) and cook in salted boiling water for about 2-4 minutes, or until al dente.

Paella

Ingredients:

- 2 tablespoons olive oil
- 1 onion, chopped
- 1 bell pepper, chopped
- 2 cloves garlic, minced
- 1 1/2 cups Arborio rice
- 1/2 cup white wine
- 3 cups chicken or vegetable broth (hot)
- 1/2 teaspoon saffron threads
- 1 teaspoon smoked paprika
- 1/2 pound chicken thighs, bone-in and skinless, chopped
- 1/2 pound shrimp, peeled and deveined
- 1/2 pound mussels or clams
- 1/2 pound chorizo, sliced
- 1/2 cup frozen peas
- Salt and pepper to taste
- Lemon wedges (for garnish)
- Fresh parsley (for garnish)

Instructions:

1. Heat olive oil in a large paella pan or wide skillet over medium heat. Add the onion, bell pepper, and garlic. Sauté until softened, about 5 minutes.
2. Add the rice and stir to coat in the oil and vegetables for 1-2 minutes.
3. Pour in the white wine, stirring until absorbed.
4. Stir in the hot broth, saffron, and paprika. Bring to a simmer.
5. Add the chicken and chorizo, distributing evenly across the pan.
6. Let the mixture simmer gently, without stirring, for about 10 minutes.
7. Add the shrimp, mussels, and peas. Continue cooking for another 10-15 minutes, or until the rice is tender and the seafood is cooked through. If the liquid evaporates before the rice is done, add a bit more broth or water.
8. Season with salt and pepper to taste.
9. Garnish with fresh parsley and lemon wedges before serving.

Dim Sum

Ingredients:

- 1 package of dumpling wrappers
- 1/2 lb ground pork or chicken
- 2 tablespoons soy sauce
- 1 tablespoon oyster sauce
- 1 teaspoon sesame oil
- 1 tablespoon grated ginger
- 1 garlic clove, minced
- 1/4 cup finely chopped green onions
- 1/4 cup finely chopped water chestnuts or bamboo shoots (optional)

Instructions:

1. In a mixing bowl, combine the ground pork or chicken with soy sauce, oyster sauce, sesame oil, ginger, garlic, green onions, and water chestnuts (if using).
2. Place a teaspoon of the filling in the center of each dumpling wrapper.
3. Fold and pinch the edges to form a dumpling. You can pleat the edges for a traditional look.
4. Steam the dumplings in a bamboo or metal steamer for about 10-12 minutes, until fully cooked.
5. Serve with soy sauce, vinegar, or chili oil for dipping.

Ramen from Scratch

Ingredients:

- 2 cups all-purpose flour
- 2 teaspoons baking soda
- 1/2 teaspoon salt
- 1/2 cup warm water
- 2 eggs
- 1 tablespoon vegetable oil
- 6 cups chicken or vegetable broth
- 1 tablespoon soy sauce
- 1 teaspoon miso paste
- 2 garlic cloves, minced
- 1 tablespoon ginger, minced
- 1/2 cup sliced mushrooms
- 2 boiled eggs (for garnish)
- Scallions (for garnish)
- Nori seaweed (for garnish)

Instructions:

1. In a bowl, mix flour, baking soda, and salt. Add eggs, oil, and warm water. Mix until the dough comes together.
2. Knead the dough on a floured surface for about 10 minutes until smooth. Cover and let rest for 30 minutes.
3. Roll out the dough and cut it into thin noodles.
4. Bring a large pot of water to a boil and cook the noodles for about 4-5 minutes until tender.
5. In another pot, combine chicken or vegetable broth, soy sauce, miso paste, garlic, ginger, and mushrooms. Simmer for 15 minutes.
6. Serve the noodles in a bowl, pour the broth over, and garnish with boiled eggs, scallions, and nori.

Beef Wellington

Ingredients:

- 2 lb beef tenderloin (center-cut)
- 2 tablespoons olive oil
- Salt and pepper to taste
- 2 tablespoons Dijon mustard
- 1 lb mushrooms, finely chopped
- 1 tablespoon butter
- 1/4 cup heavy cream
- 1 sheet puff pastry
- 2 egg yolks (for egg wash)
- 1/4 lb prosciutto

Instructions:

1. Preheat oven to 400°F (200°C).
2. Season the beef tenderloin with salt and pepper. Heat olive oil in a pan over high heat and sear the beef on all sides until browned. Let it cool, then brush with Dijon mustard.
3. In the same pan, melt butter and sauté the chopped mushrooms until all moisture evaporates, leaving a dry mixture. Add cream and cook until thickened. Let cool.
4. Roll out the puff pastry and place the prosciutto on top. Spread the mushroom mixture over the prosciutto.
5. Place the beef in the center and wrap the pastry around it. Seal the edges and brush with egg wash.
6. Bake for 40-45 minutes, or until the pastry is golden and the beef reaches your desired level of doneness.
7. Let it rest for 10 minutes before slicing and serving.

Dumplings

Ingredients:

- 1 lb ground pork or chicken
- 1 tablespoon soy sauce
- 1 tablespoon sesame oil
- 1 teaspoon grated ginger
- 2 garlic cloves, minced
- 1/4 cup finely chopped green onions
- 1/4 cup finely chopped cabbage or napa cabbage
- Dumpling wrappers
- Water for sealing

Instructions:

1. In a bowl, combine the ground pork or chicken, soy sauce, sesame oil, ginger, garlic, green onions, and cabbage. Mix until well combined.
2. Place a teaspoon of filling in the center of each dumpling wrapper.
3. Wet the edges with water and fold into a half-moon shape. Pinch the edges to seal tightly.
4. Steam the dumplings for about 8-10 minutes or until fully cooked.
5. Serve with soy sauce, vinegar, and chili oil for dipping.

Thai Green Curry

Ingredients:

- 1 tablespoon vegetable oil
- 1 tablespoon green curry paste
- 1 can (14 oz) coconut milk
- 2 cups chicken broth
- 1 lb chicken breast, thinly sliced
- 1 cup bell peppers, sliced
- 1 cup zucchini, sliced
- 1/4 cup fish sauce
- 1 tablespoon brown sugar
- 1/2 cup basil leaves

Instructions:

1. Heat vegetable oil in a large pan over medium heat. Add green curry paste and cook for 1-2 minutes until fragrant.
2. Add coconut milk, chicken broth, chicken, bell peppers, and zucchini. Simmer for 15 minutes until the chicken is cooked.
3. Stir in fish sauce, brown sugar, and basil leaves. Simmer for another 2 minutes.
4. Serve with jasmine rice.

Moussaka

Ingredients:

- 2 eggplants, sliced
- 2 tablespoons olive oil
- 1 lb ground lamb or beef
- 1 onion, chopped
- 2 garlic cloves, minced
- 1 can (14 oz) diced tomatoes
- 1 teaspoon ground cinnamon
- 1/4 teaspoon ground nutmeg
- 1/2 cup red wine
- 1/4 cup chopped parsley
- 1/2 cup grated Parmesan cheese
- 2 cups béchamel sauce (butter, flour, milk, nutmeg, and cheese)

Instructions:

1. Preheat the oven to 375°F (190°C).
2. Slice the eggplants and brush with olive oil. Roast in the oven for 25-30 minutes until tender.
3. In a pan, brown the ground meat with onion and garlic. Add tomatoes, cinnamon, nutmeg, red wine, and parsley. Simmer for 15 minutes.
4. In a baking dish, layer the eggplant slices, followed by the meat mixture, and top with béchamel sauce.
5. Sprinkle Parmesan on top and bake for 30-35 minutes until golden and bubbly.

Croissants

Ingredients:

- 4 cups all-purpose flour
- 1/2 cup water
- 1/2 cup milk
- 1/4 cup sugar
- 2 teaspoons salt
- 2 tablespoons yeast
- 1 cup unsalted butter, cold and cut into cubes
- 1 egg (for egg wash)

Instructions:

1. In a bowl, combine warm water, milk, sugar, and yeast. Let it sit for 5 minutes to activate the yeast.
2. Mix in the flour and salt to form a dough. Knead for 5-7 minutes until smooth. Let it rise for 1 hour.
3. Roll the dough into a rectangle. Place cold butter in the center and fold the dough around it. Roll out and fold the dough over itself three times to create layers.
4. Chill the dough for 30 minutes between folds. After the final fold, roll out and cut into triangles.
5. Roll each triangle from the base to the tip and form a crescent shape.
6. Let the croissants rise for 2 hours, then brush with an egg wash.
7. Bake at 375°F (190°C) for 20-25 minutes until golden brown.

Chicken Shawarma

Ingredients:

- 1 lb chicken thighs (boneless, skinless)
- 2 tablespoons olive oil
- 1 tablespoon ground cumin
- 1 tablespoon paprika
- 1 teaspoon turmeric
- 1 teaspoon ground coriander
- 1/2 teaspoon cinnamon
- 3 garlic cloves, minced
- 1 tablespoon lemon juice
- Salt and pepper to taste
- Pita bread or flatbread
- Toppings: lettuce, tomatoes, cucumbers, tahini sauce

Instructions:

1. In a bowl, mix olive oil, cumin, paprika, turmeric, coriander, cinnamon, garlic, lemon juice, salt, and pepper.
2. Marinate the chicken thighs in the spice mixture for at least 1 hour (preferably overnight).
3. Grill or pan-fry the chicken over medium heat until cooked through (about 6-7 minutes per side).
4. Slice the chicken thinly and serve in pita bread with lettuce, tomatoes, cucumbers, and tahini sauce.

Korean BBQ

Ingredients:

- 1 lb beef short ribs or bulgogi beef slices
- 1/4 cup soy sauce
- 2 tablespoons sesame oil
- 1 tablespoon rice vinegar
- 2 tablespoons brown sugar
- 3 cloves garlic, minced
- 1 tablespoon ginger, minced
- 2 tablespoons gochujang (Korean chili paste)
- 1 tablespoon sesame seeds
- 2 scallions, chopped
- Cooked rice and lettuce leaves for serving

Instructions:

1. In a bowl, combine soy sauce, sesame oil, rice vinegar, brown sugar, garlic, ginger, and gochujang. Whisk until smooth.
2. Marinate the beef in the mixture for at least 30 minutes.
3. Grill the beef for 2-3 minutes per side.
4. Garnish with sesame seeds and scallions, then serve with rice and lettuce leaves.

Tagine

Ingredients:

- 1 lb chicken thighs or lamb (bone-in or boneless)
- 2 tablespoons olive oil
- 1 onion, chopped
- 2 garlic cloves, minced
- 1 teaspoon ground cumin
- 1 teaspoon ground ginger
- 1 teaspoon paprika
- 1/2 teaspoon ground turmeric
- 1/4 teaspoon cinnamon
- 1/2 cup dried apricots, chopped
- 1/2 cup green olives, pitted and chopped
- 1 can (14 oz) diced tomatoes
- 1 cup chicken broth
- 1 tablespoon honey
- Salt and pepper to taste
- Fresh cilantro, chopped (for garnish)

Instructions:

1. In a large tagine or heavy-bottomed pot, heat olive oil over medium heat. Brown the chicken or lamb on all sides. Remove and set aside.
2. In the same pot, sauté the onion and garlic until softened.
3. Stir in cumin, ginger, paprika, turmeric, and cinnamon. Cook for 1-2 minutes until fragrant.
4. Return the chicken or lamb to the pot. Add the chopped apricots, olives, diced tomatoes, chicken broth, and honey. Season with salt and pepper.
5. Cover and simmer on low for 1-1.5 hours, until the meat is tender and the flavors meld together.
6. Garnish with fresh cilantro before serving. Serve with couscous or rice.

Homemade Tortillas

Ingredients:

- 2 cups all-purpose flour
- 1 teaspoon baking powder
- 1/2 teaspoon salt
- 1/4 cup vegetable oil
- 3/4 cup warm water (more if needed)

Instructions:

1. In a large bowl, combine flour, baking powder, and salt. Add vegetable oil and mix until the dough resembles coarse crumbs.
2. Gradually add warm water, stirring until a dough forms. Knead the dough for 3-5 minutes until smooth.
3. Divide the dough into 8 equal balls. Let them rest for 10 minutes.
4. Roll each ball into a thin circle on a floured surface.
5. Heat a skillet over medium-high heat. Cook each tortilla for about 1-2 minutes per side, until lightly browned and cooked through.
6. Serve warm.

Sushi Burritos

Ingredients:

- 2 cups sushi rice, cooked
- 2 tablespoons rice vinegar
- 1 tablespoon sugar
- 1 teaspoon salt
- 4 large seaweed sheets (nori)
- 1/2 lb sushi-grade tuna or salmon, sliced thin
- 1/2 avocado, sliced
- 1/2 cucumber, julienned
- 1/4 cup shredded carrots
- Soy sauce, for dipping
- Wasabi and pickled ginger (optional)

Instructions:

1. In a small bowl, combine rice vinegar, sugar, and salt. Stir until dissolved. Mix into the cooked rice.
2. Lay a sheet of nori on a flat surface, shiny side down. Spread a thin layer of rice evenly over the nori, leaving 1 inch at the top.
3. Arrange tuna or salmon, avocado, cucumber, and carrots in the center of the rice.
4. Roll the sushi tightly, folding in the sides as you go. Seal the edge with a little water.
5. Slice the sushi burrito in half and serve with soy sauce, wasabi, and pickled ginger.

Empanadas

Ingredients:

- 1 lb ground beef or chicken
- 1 onion, chopped
- 1 garlic clove, minced
- 1 teaspoon cumin
- 1/2 teaspoon paprika
- 1/2 cup olives, chopped
- 1/4 cup raisins (optional)
- 1/4 cup hard-boiled eggs, chopped
- 1 package empanada dough discs (or make your own)
- 1 egg (for egg wash)
- Vegetable oil (for frying)

Instructions:

1. In a pan, cook the ground meat with onion and garlic until browned.
2. Stir in cumin, paprika, olives, raisins, and hard-boiled eggs. Cook for another 2 minutes. Let the filling cool.
3. Preheat the oven to 375°F (190°C).
4. Place a spoonful of filling in the center of each empanada disc. Fold over and crimp the edges to seal.
5. Brush with egg wash and bake for 20-25 minutes, or until golden brown.
6. Serve with a dipping sauce of your choice.

Risotto

Ingredients:

- 1 cup Arborio rice
- 4 cups chicken or vegetable broth
- 1/2 cup white wine (optional)
- 1/2 onion, chopped
- 2 garlic cloves, minced
- 2 tablespoons olive oil or butter
- 1/2 cup Parmesan cheese, grated
- Salt and pepper to taste

Instructions:

1. In a saucepan, heat the broth over low heat.
2. In another pan, sauté onion and garlic in olive oil or butter until softened.
3. Add the rice and stir to coat. Pour in the wine and let it cook off.
4. Gradually add the warm broth, 1/2 cup at a time, stirring constantly until the liquid is absorbed before adding more.
5. Continue adding broth and stirring until the rice is creamy and cooked through (about 20 minutes).
6. Stir in Parmesan cheese and season with salt and pepper. Serve immediately.

Pho

Ingredients:

- 1 lb beef brisket or chicken (bone-in)
- 2-inch piece of ginger, sliced
- 2-3 cloves garlic, smashed
- 1 onion, halved
- 4 cups beef or chicken broth
- 1 cinnamon stick
- 2-3 star anise
- 3-4 whole cloves
- 1 tablespoon fish sauce
- 1 tablespoon sugar
- 2 cups rice noodles
- Fresh basil, cilantro, lime wedges, and bean sprouts for garnish

Instructions:

1. In a large pot, add the meat, ginger, garlic, and onion. Cover with water and bring to a boil. Reduce heat and simmer for 1-1.5 hours for beef or 30 minutes for chicken.
2. Remove the meat and set aside. Strain the broth and return it to the pot.
3. Add the cinnamon stick, star anise, cloves, fish sauce, and sugar. Simmer for another 30 minutes.
4. Cook the rice noodles according to package instructions.
5. Slice the cooked meat thinly. Serve the broth over the noodles and top with meat, basil, cilantro, lime, and bean sprouts.

Tacos al Pastor

Ingredients:

- 2 lbs pork shoulder, thinly sliced
- 1/4 cup pineapple juice
- 1/4 cup orange juice
- 2 tablespoons vinegar
- 1 tablespoon adobo sauce (from canned chipotles)
- 1 tablespoon ground cumin
- 1 tablespoon chili powder
- 1 teaspoon ground oregano
- Salt and pepper to taste
- 1/2 pineapple, sliced
- Small corn tortillas
- Onion, cilantro, lime wedges for garnish

Instructions:

1. In a bowl, combine pineapple juice, orange juice, vinegar, adobo sauce, cumin, chili powder, oregano, salt, and pepper.
2. Marinate the pork slices in the mixture for at least 2 hours, preferably overnight.
3. Preheat a grill or skillet. Grill the marinated pork slices and pineapple until cooked through.
4. Slice the pork and pineapple thinly. Serve on warm tortillas, garnished with onion, cilantro, and lime.

Jambalaya

Ingredients:

- 1 lb chicken thighs, chopped
- 1 lb shrimp, peeled and deveined
- 1/2 lb sausage, sliced (Andouille or smoked sausage)
- 1 onion, chopped
- 1 bell pepper, chopped
- 2 celery stalks, chopped
- 3 garlic cloves, minced
- 1 can (14 oz) diced tomatoes
- 2 cups chicken broth
- 2 cups long-grain rice
- 1 teaspoon thyme
- 1 teaspoon paprika
- 1/2 teaspoon cayenne pepper
- Salt and pepper to taste
- 2 tablespoons vegetable oil

Instructions:

1. In a large pot, heat vegetable oil over medium heat. Brown the chicken and sausage, then remove and set aside.
2. In the same pot, sauté onion, bell pepper, celery, and garlic until softened.
3. Add the rice, tomatoes, chicken broth, thyme, paprika, cayenne, salt, and pepper. Stir to combine.
4. Bring to a boil, then reduce heat and cover. Simmer for 20 minutes.
5. Add the shrimp and cooked chicken back into the pot. Cook for another 5 minutes, until the shrimp are cooked through.
6. Serve hot.

Tamales

Ingredients:

- 2 cups masa harina
- 1 cup chicken broth
- 1/2 cup vegetable oil or lard
- 1 teaspoon baking powder
- 1 teaspoon salt
- 2 cups cooked chicken or pork, shredded
- 1/2 cup red chile sauce (or salsa)
- Corn husks (soaked in warm water)

Instructions:

1. In a bowl, combine masa harina, baking powder, salt, and vegetable oil or lard. Gradually add chicken broth, mixing until smooth and dough-like.
2. Spread a spoonful of masa dough onto a corn husk.
3. Top with a spoonful of shredded chicken or pork and red chile sauce.
4. Fold the sides of the husk over the filling and roll it up.
5. Steam the tamales in a large steamer for 1-1.5 hours, until the masa is cooked through.
6. Serve with extra salsa or crema.

Kimchi

Ingredients:

- 1 medium napa cabbage
- 1/4 cup salt
- 3 cups water
- 1 tablespoon grated ginger
- 5 cloves garlic, minced
- 2 tablespoons fish sauce
- 1 tablespoon sugar
- 2 tablespoons gochugaru (Korean red pepper flakes)
- 1/4 cup sliced green onions

Instructions:

1. Cut the cabbage into quarters and remove the core. Slice into bite-sized pieces. Soak the cabbage in salted water for 2-3 hours.
2. Rinse and drain the cabbage thoroughly.
3. In a bowl, mix ginger, garlic, fish sauce, sugar, gochugaru, and green onions. Stir to form a paste.
4. Massage the paste into the cabbage, making sure it's evenly coated.
5. Pack the kimchi into a jar, pressing it down to release air bubbles.
6. Let it ferment at room temperature for 1-2 days, then refrigerate for up to a week.

Gnocchi

Ingredients:

- 2 lbs potatoes (Yukon Gold or Russet)
- 2 cups all-purpose flour, plus extra for dusting
- 1 large egg
- Salt to taste
- Freshly grated Parmesan (for serving)

Instructions:

1. Boil the potatoes with their skins on until tender (about 20-25 minutes). Drain and peel while still warm.
2. Mash the potatoes and let them cool slightly. Combine with flour, egg, and a pinch of salt. Mix until smooth dough forms.
3. Roll the dough into long ropes, then cut into 1-inch pieces. Use a fork to press gently into each piece to form the gnocchi indentations.
4. Bring a pot of salted water to a boil. Drop the gnocchi into the water in batches. Once they float to the surface, cook for an additional 2-3 minutes.
5. Serve with your favorite sauce and freshly grated Parmesan.

Banh Mi

Ingredients:

- 1 French baguette (or crusty sandwich roll)
- 1/2 lb pork (or chicken, tofu for a vegetarian version), thinly sliced
- 1 tablespoon soy sauce
- 1 tablespoon fish sauce
- 1 teaspoon sugar
- 1 tablespoon mayonnaise
- 1 tablespoon sriracha sauce
- 1/4 cup cucumber, thinly sliced
- 1/4 cup cilantro leaves
- 1/4 cup pickled carrots and daikon (recipe below)
- Jalapeno slices (optional)
- Salt and pepper to taste

Instructions:

1. Marinate the meat (pork, chicken, or tofu) in soy sauce, fish sauce, and sugar for at least 30 minutes.
2. Mix mayonnaise with sriracha sauce. Set aside.
3. Grill or pan-fry the marinated meat until fully cooked.
4. Cut the baguette in half and lightly toast if desired.
5. Spread mayonnaise-sriracha mixture on both halves of the baguette.
6. Layer the grilled meat, pickled vegetables, cucumber, cilantro, and jalapenos (if using) inside the baguette.
7. Serve immediately!

Pickled Carrots and Daikon:

- 1/2 cup shredded carrots
- 1/2 cup shredded daikon radish
- 1/4 cup rice vinegar
- 1 tablespoon sugar
- 1/4 teaspoon salt
    - Combine ingredients and let sit for at least 30 minutes before using.

Burrata with Roasted Veggies

Ingredients:

- 1 ball of burrata cheese
- 1 zucchini, sliced
- 1 eggplant, sliced
- 1 bell pepper, sliced
- 1 red onion, sliced
- 2 tablespoons olive oil
- 1 teaspoon dried oregano
- Salt and pepper to taste
- Fresh basil leaves (for garnish)
- Balsamic glaze (optional)

Instructions:

1. Preheat the oven to 400°F (200°C).
2. Toss the sliced vegetables with olive oil, oregano, salt, and pepper. Spread them evenly on a baking sheet.
3. Roast the vegetables for 20-25 minutes, flipping halfway, until tender and caramelized.
4. Plate the roasted veggies and top with burrata cheese. Drizzle with balsamic glaze (optional) and garnish with fresh basil.
5. Serve immediately.

Paella Valenciana

Ingredients:

- 2 tablespoons olive oil
- 1/2 lb chicken thighs, boneless and cut into pieces
- 1/2 lb rabbit (optional), cut into pieces
- 1 onion, chopped
- 1 bell pepper, chopped
- 2 garlic cloves, minced
- 1 1/2 cups Bomba rice (or Arborio rice)
- 1/2 teaspoon saffron threads
- 4 cups chicken or vegetable broth
- 1 cup peas (frozen or fresh)
- 1 tomato, chopped
- 1 teaspoon paprika
- Salt and pepper to taste
- 1/2 lb shrimp, peeled and deveined
- 1/2 lb mussels (optional)

Instructions:

1. In a large paella pan or wide skillet, heat olive oil over medium heat. Brown the chicken and rabbit pieces. Remove and set aside.
2. In the same pan, sauté onion, bell pepper, and garlic until softened.
3. Add rice and saffron, stir to coat the rice with the oil and vegetables.
4. Add broth, peas, tomato, paprika, salt, and pepper. Bring to a simmer.
5. Return the chicken and rabbit to the pan. Cover and cook for 15-20 minutes until the rice is nearly tender.
6. Add shrimp and mussels. Cover and cook for an additional 5-10 minutes, until the shrimp is cooked and the mussels have opened.
7. Serve the paella straight from the pan with lemon wedges.

Ceviche

Ingredients:

- 1 lb fresh fish (such as tilapia, halibut, or shrimp), diced
- 1/2 red onion, finely chopped
- 1 cucumber, diced
- 1/2 cup chopped cilantro
- 1 jalapeno, minced (optional)
- 1/4 cup fresh lime juice
- 1/4 cup fresh lemon juice
- Salt and pepper to taste

Instructions:

1. Combine the diced fish with lime and lemon juice. The acid will "cook" the fish.
2. Let the mixture sit for 2-3 hours in the refrigerator, stirring occasionally.
3. Add the red onion, cucumber, cilantro, and jalapeno (if using).
4. Season with salt and pepper to taste. Serve chilled with tortilla chips or on tostadas.

Chicken Kiev

Ingredients:

- 4 boneless, skinless chicken breasts
- 1/2 cup unsalted butter, softened
- 2 cloves garlic, minced
- 2 tablespoons fresh parsley, chopped
- 1 tablespoon fresh dill, chopped
- 1 teaspoon lemon zest
- Salt and pepper to taste
- 1/2 cup all-purpose flour
- 1/2 cup breadcrumbs
- 1 large egg, beaten
- Vegetable oil for frying

Instructions:

1. For the filling, mix softened butter, garlic, parsley, dill, lemon zest, salt, and pepper. Roll into a log and refrigerate until firm.
2. Carefully make a pocket in each chicken breast. Insert a piece of the garlic butter mixture into each pocket, sealing the edges with toothpicks.
3. Dredge the chicken in flour, then dip into the egg and coat in breadcrumbs.
4. Heat oil in a pan over medium-high heat. Fry the chicken for 4-5 minutes per side, until golden brown and cooked through.
5. Serve immediately, garnished with additional parsley.

Coq au Vin

Ingredients:

- 1 whole chicken, cut into pieces
- 2 tablespoons olive oil
- 1 onion, chopped
- 2 carrots, chopped
- 2 celery stalks, chopped
- 3 garlic cloves, minced
- 1 cup red wine
- 2 cups chicken broth
- 1 bouquet garni (thyme, rosemary, bay leaves)
- 1/2 lb mushrooms, sliced
- 1/4 cup chopped fresh parsley
- Salt and pepper to taste

Instructions:

1. Heat olive oil in a large pot over medium heat. Brown the chicken pieces on all sides and set aside.
2. In the same pot, sauté the onion, carrots, celery, and garlic until softened.
3. Return the chicken to the pot, add wine, chicken broth, and bouquet garni. Bring to a boil, then reduce heat and simmer for 45 minutes to an hour.
4. In a separate pan, sauté the mushrooms until browned. Add them to the pot and cook for another 10-15 minutes.
5. Remove the bouquet garni, season with salt and pepper, and sprinkle with fresh parsley before serving.

Shakshuka

Ingredients:

- 2 tablespoons olive oil
- 1 onion, chopped
- 1 bell pepper, chopped
- 2 garlic cloves, minced
- 1 can (14 oz) crushed tomatoes
- 1 teaspoon cumin
- 1 teaspoon paprika
- 1/2 teaspoon chili flakes (optional)
- 4-6 eggs
- Salt and pepper to taste
- Fresh cilantro, chopped (for garnish)

Instructions:

1. Heat olive oil in a large pan over medium heat. Sauté the onion, bell pepper, and garlic until softened.
2. Add the crushed tomatoes, cumin, paprika, and chili flakes. Simmer for 15-20 minutes, until the sauce thickens.
3. Make small wells in the sauce and crack eggs into each well.
4. Cover the pan and cook until the eggs are set, about 5-7 minutes.
5. Season with salt and pepper and garnish with fresh cilantro. Serve with pita bread or crusty bread.

Peking Duck

Ingredients:

- 1 whole duck (about 4-5 lbs)
- 2 tablespoons Chinese five-spice powder
- 1/4 cup honey
- 2 tablespoons rice vinegar
- 1/4 cup soy sauce
- 1 tablespoon hoisin sauce
- 1/4 teaspoon salt

Instructions:

1. Preheat the oven to 375°F (190°C). Prick the duck skin with a fork to allow the fat to render.
2. Mix five-spice powder, honey, rice vinegar, soy sauce, hoisin sauce, and salt to form a glaze.
3. Rub the glaze over the duck and roast for 1.5-2 hours, basting occasionally with the glaze.
4. Let the duck rest before slicing. Serve with pancakes, hoisin sauce, and sliced scallions.

Beef and Ale Pie

Ingredients:

- 1 lb beef stew meat, cubed
- 2 tablespoons olive oil
- 1 onion, chopped
- 2 carrots, chopped
- 2 cloves garlic, minced
- 2 tablespoons tomato paste
- 1 1/2 cups ale (preferably a dark beer)
- 1 cup beef broth
- 2 teaspoons dried thyme
- 1 teaspoon Worcestershire sauce
- 1 sheet puff pastry (or homemade pie dough)
- 1 egg (for egg wash)
- Salt and pepper to taste

Instructions:

1. In a large pot, heat olive oil over medium heat. Brown the beef in batches, then set aside.
2. In the same pot, sauté onion, carrots, and garlic until softened.
3. Add tomato paste and cook for 1-2 minutes, then add the ale, beef broth, thyme, and Worcestershire sauce. Bring to a boil.
4. Return the beef to the pot and simmer for 1.5-2 hours, or until the beef is tender.
5. Preheat the oven to 375°F (190°C). Transfer the beef mixture to a pie dish.
6. Roll out the puff pastry and cover the pie. Brush with a beaten egg for a golden crust.
7. Bake for 30-35 minutes, or until the pastry is golden and puffed. Serve hot.

Ravioli from Scratch

Ingredients for Pasta Dough:

- 2 cups all-purpose flour
- 3 large eggs
- 1 tablespoon olive oil
- 1/2 teaspoon salt

Ingredients for Filling:

- 1/2 lb ricotta cheese
- 1/2 cup grated Parmesan cheese
- 1/2 teaspoon nutmeg
- Salt and pepper to taste

Instructions:

1. To make the dough, mound flour on a clean surface, create a well in the center, and crack eggs into the well. Add olive oil and salt.
2. Gently mix the eggs with a fork, gradually incorporating the flour, and knead until smooth, about 10 minutes. Wrap and let rest for 30 minutes.
3. For the filling, mix ricotta, Parmesan, nutmeg, salt, and pepper.
4. Roll out the dough into thin sheets. Place small dollops of filling about 2 inches apart.
5. Fold the dough over to cover the filling, then press the edges to seal. Cut into individual ravioli.
6. Boil the ravioli in salted water for about 2-3 minutes, or until they float. Serve with your favorite sauce.

French Onion Soup

Ingredients:

- 4 large onions, thinly sliced
- 3 tablespoons butter
- 1 tablespoon olive oil
- 1 teaspoon sugar
- 2 cloves garlic, minced
- 1/2 cup dry white wine
- 4 cups beef broth
- 1 bay leaf
- 1 teaspoon fresh thyme (or 1/2 teaspoon dried thyme)
- Salt and pepper to taste
- 4 slices French baguette
- 1 1/2 cups grated Gruyère cheese

Instructions:

1. In a large pot, heat butter and olive oil over medium heat. Add onions and cook, stirring occasionally, until golden and caramelized, about 30-40 minutes. Sprinkle with sugar to help with caramelization.
2. Add garlic and cook for another minute. Deglaze the pot with white wine.
3. Add the beef broth, bay leaf, thyme, salt, and pepper. Simmer for 30 minutes.
4. Preheat the broiler. Toast the baguette slices until golden.
5. Ladle the soup into oven-safe bowls, top with a toasted baguette slice, and sprinkle with Gruyère cheese.
6. Place under the broiler for 2-3 minutes, until the cheese is melted and bubbly. Serve hot.

Samosas

Ingredients for Filling:

- 2 tablespoons vegetable oil
- 1 onion, chopped
- 2 cloves garlic, minced
- 2 tablespoons ginger, grated
- 2 cups cooked potatoes, mashed
- 1/2 cup frozen peas
- 1 teaspoon cumin
- 1 teaspoon coriander
- 1/2 teaspoon turmeric
- 1/4 teaspoon garam masala
- 1/2 teaspoon chili powder (optional)
- Salt to taste
- Fresh cilantro, chopped

Ingredients for Dough:

- 2 cups all-purpose flour
- 1/4 cup vegetable oil
- 1/2 teaspoon salt
- Water (as needed)

Instructions:

1. Heat oil in a pan over medium heat. Sauté onions, garlic, and ginger until softened.
2. Add the spices and cook for another minute, then add mashed potatoes, peas, and salt. Stir in cilantro and remove from heat.
3. To make the dough, mix flour, salt, and oil in a bowl. Gradually add water and knead into a smooth dough. Let rest for 30 minutes.
4. Roll the dough into thin circles, then cut in half. Form a cone shape with each half and fill with the potato mixture.
5. Seal the edges, pinching to form a triangle.
6. Heat oil in a pan and fry the samosas in batches until golden and crisp. Drain on paper towels and serve with chutney.

Tarte Tatin

Ingredients:

- 6-8 medium apples (preferably Golden Delicious or Granny Smith)
- 1/2 cup unsalted butter
- 1 cup granulated sugar
- 1 sheet puff pastry (or homemade pie dough)
- Cinnamon (optional)

Instructions:

1. Preheat the oven to 375°F (190°C).
2. Peel, core, and slice apples.
3. In an oven-safe skillet, melt butter over medium heat and add sugar. Cook until the sugar dissolves and begins to caramelize.
4. Arrange the apple slices in the skillet in a circular pattern, filling gaps as necessary. Cook for 10-15 minutes until the apples are tender.
5. Roll out the puff pastry and place over the apples, tucking the edges around the sides.
6. Bake for 25-30 minutes until the pastry is golden brown.
7. Allow to cool for a few minutes before inverting onto a plate. Serve warm.

Risotto alla Milanese

Ingredients:

- 2 tablespoons butter
- 1 tablespoon olive oil
- 1 small onion, finely chopped
- 1 1/2 cups Arborio rice
- 1/2 cup dry white wine
- 4 cups chicken or vegetable broth, kept warm
- 1/2 teaspoon saffron threads
- 1/2 cup grated Parmesan cheese
- Salt and pepper to taste

Instructions:

1. In a large pan, heat butter and olive oil over medium heat. Add onion and cook until softened.
2. Add rice and cook for 1-2 minutes, stirring frequently to coat the rice in the oil and butter.
3. Pour in the wine and stir until absorbed.
4. Add the warm broth, one ladle at a time, stirring frequently. Wait until most of the liquid is absorbed before adding more broth.
5. After 15-20 minutes, the rice should be tender. Stir in saffron, Parmesan, salt, and pepper. Serve immediately.

Croque Monsieur

Ingredients:

- 4 slices white bread
- 2 tablespoons Dijon mustard
- 4 slices ham
- 1 cup grated Gruyère cheese
- 2 tablespoons butter
- 1/4 cup béchamel sauce (recipe below)

Instructions:

1. Preheat the broiler. Spread mustard on two slices of bread.
2. Layer each with a slice of ham and a generous amount of cheese.
3. Top with the remaining slices of bread, then spread butter on the outer sides of the bread.
4. Toast in a pan until golden, about 2 minutes per side.
5. Spread béchamel sauce on top of each sandwich and sprinkle with extra cheese.
6. Place under the broiler for 2-3 minutes until the cheese is melted and bubbly. Serve hot.

Béchamel Sauce:

- 2 tablespoons butter
- 2 tablespoons all-purpose flour
- 1 cup milk
- Salt and pepper to taste
    - Melt butter, whisk in flour, and cook for 1 minute. Gradually add milk, whisking continuously. Cook until thickened.

Sautéed Frog Legs

Ingredients:

- 1 lb frog legs
- 3 tablespoons butter
- 2 cloves garlic, minced
- 1/4 cup white wine
- 1 tablespoon fresh parsley, chopped
- Salt and pepper to taste

Instructions:

1. Rinse and pat dry the frog legs.
2. In a pan, melt butter over medium heat. Add garlic and sauté for 1 minute.
3. Add frog legs and cook for 4-5 minutes per side until golden brown.
4. Add white wine and cook for an additional 2-3 minutes until the sauce reduces.
5. Season with salt, pepper, and fresh parsley. Serve immediately.

Ratatouille

Ingredients:

- 1 eggplant, diced
- 1 zucchini, diced
- 1 bell pepper, diced
- 2 tomatoes, chopped
- 1 onion, chopped
- 2 cloves garlic, minced
- 2 tablespoons olive oil
- 1 teaspoon dried thyme
- Salt and pepper to taste

Instructions:

1. Heat olive oil in a large pan over medium heat. Sauté onions and garlic until softened.
2. Add eggplant, zucchini, and bell pepper. Cook for 5-7 minutes until vegetables are tender.
3. Add tomatoes, thyme, salt, and pepper. Simmer for 10 minutes until the vegetables are fully cooked.
4. Serve warm, garnished with fresh basil or parsley.

Mussels in White Wine Sauce

Ingredients:

- 2 lbs fresh mussels, cleaned and debearded
- 2 tablespoons olive oil
- 2 cloves garlic, minced
- 1 shallot, chopped
- 1/2 cup dry white wine
- 1 cup heavy cream
- 2 tablespoons butter
- 1 tablespoon fresh parsley, chopped
- Salt and pepper to taste

Instructions:

1. In a large pot, heat olive oil over medium heat. Add garlic and shallots, sautéing until softened.
2. Pour in the white wine and bring to a boil. Add the mussels and cover the pot. Cook for 5-7 minutes, or until the mussels open.
3. Remove the mussels from the pot and set aside. Add cream and butter to the sauce, stirring until combined.
4. Return the mussels to the pot and toss them in the sauce. Season with salt, pepper, and fresh parsley.
5. Serve immediately with crusty bread.

Szechuan Stir-fry

Ingredients:

- 1 lb chicken breast or beef, thinly sliced
- 2 tablespoons vegetable oil
- 2 cloves garlic, minced
- 1-inch ginger, minced
- 1 bell pepper, sliced
- 1 carrot, julienned
- 2 tablespoons soy sauce
- 2 tablespoons rice vinegar
- 1 tablespoon Szechuan peppercorns
- 2 tablespoons chili paste
- 1 tablespoon hoisin sauce
- Cooked rice, for serving

Instructions:

1. Heat vegetable oil in a wok or large skillet over medium-high heat. Add garlic, ginger, and Szechuan peppercorns, cooking until fragrant.
2. Add chicken or beef to the pan and cook until browned.
3. Add the bell pepper and carrot, cooking for 2-3 minutes.
4. Stir in soy sauce, rice vinegar, chili paste, and hoisin sauce. Cook for another 2 minutes, ensuring the sauce coats the ingredients.
5. Serve over rice, garnished with additional chili paste or green onions if desired.

Frittata

Ingredients:

- 8 large eggs
- 1/4 cup milk
- 1 tablespoon olive oil
- 1 onion, chopped
- 1 bell pepper, chopped
- 1 zucchini, chopped
- 1/2 cup cheese (cheddar, feta, or goat cheese)
- Salt and pepper to taste

Instructions:

1. Preheat the oven to 375°F (190°C).
2. In a bowl, whisk together eggs, milk, salt, and pepper.
3. Heat olive oil in an oven-safe skillet over medium heat. Sauté onion, bell pepper, and zucchini until softened, about 5-7 minutes.
4. Pour the egg mixture into the skillet, stirring gently to distribute the vegetables evenly.
5. Sprinkle cheese over the top and transfer the skillet to the oven.
6. Bake for 10-12 minutes, or until the eggs are set. Serve warm.

Bouillabaisse

Ingredients:

- 1 lb firm white fish (such as cod or snapper), cut into chunks
- 1/2 lb shellfish (such as shrimp or mussels), cleaned
- 2 tablespoons olive oil
- 1 onion, chopped
- 2 leeks, cleaned and sliced
- 2 tomatoes, chopped
- 3 cloves garlic, minced
- 1 teaspoon saffron
- 4 cups fish stock
- 1/2 cup white wine
- 1 tablespoon tomato paste
- Salt and pepper to taste
- Fresh basil, for garnish
- Crusty bread, for serving

Instructions:

1. In a large pot, heat olive oil over medium heat. Add onions, leeks, and garlic, cooking until softened.
2. Add tomatoes, saffron, fish stock, white wine, and tomato paste. Bring to a simmer.
3. Add fish and shellfish to the pot and cook for 10-12 minutes, or until the fish is cooked through.
4. Season with salt and pepper to taste. Serve the bouillabaisse with crusty bread and garnish with fresh basil.

Bangers and Mash

Ingredients:

- 6 sausages (preferably pork or beef)
- 2 pounds potatoes, peeled and cubed
- 4 tablespoons butter
- 1/2 cup milk
- 1/2 cup beef broth
- 1 tablespoon flour
- 1 tablespoon Worcestershire sauce
- Salt and pepper to taste

Instructions:

1. Cook the sausages in a skillet over medium heat until browned and cooked through, about 10 minutes.
2. Boil the potatoes in salted water until tender, about 15 minutes. Drain and mash with butter and milk. Season with salt and pepper.
3. For the gravy, melt butter in the skillet, then whisk in flour. Cook for 1-2 minutes before adding beef broth and Worcestershire sauce. Simmer until thickened.
4. Serve sausages over mashed potatoes, topped with gravy.

Arancini

Ingredients:

- 2 cups cooked risotto (preferably leftover)
- 1/2 cup mozzarella cheese, cut into small cubes
- 1/4 cup grated Parmesan cheese
- 1 egg, beaten
- 1/2 cup all-purpose flour
- 1/2 cup breadcrumbs
- Vegetable oil, for frying
- Marinara sauce, for dipping

Instructions:

1. Form the risotto into small balls, about the size of a golf ball. Press a cube of mozzarella into the center of each ball, then roll in grated Parmesan.
2. Dredge each ball in flour, dip into beaten egg, then coat with breadcrumbs.
3. Heat vegetable oil in a pan over medium heat. Fry the arancini in batches until golden brown, about 4-5 minutes.
4. Drain on paper towels and serve with marinara sauce.

Croissant Sandwiches

Ingredients:

- 4 croissants, halved
- 8 slices deli turkey or ham
- 4 slices Swiss or cheddar cheese
- 1/4 cup mayonnaise
- 1 tablespoon Dijon mustard
- Lettuce and tomato, for garnish

Instructions:

1. Preheat the oven to 350°F (175°C). Place the croissant halves on a baking sheet.
2. Spread mayonnaise and Dijon mustard on the inside of each croissant.
3. Layer with deli meat, cheese, lettuce, and tomato.
4. Bake for 5-7 minutes, or until the cheese is melted and the croissants are slightly toasted. Serve immediately.

Korma Curry

Ingredients:

- 1 lb chicken or lamb, cubed
- 2 tablespoons vegetable oil
- 1 onion, chopped
- 2 cloves garlic, minced
- 1-inch ginger, minced
- 1 tablespoon curry powder
- 1 teaspoon ground turmeric
- 1 teaspoon ground cumin
- 1/2 cup plain yogurt
- 1/2 cup heavy cream
- 1/4 cup ground almonds
- 1/2 cup chicken broth
- Salt to taste
- Fresh cilantro, for garnish
- Cooked rice, for serving

Instructions:

1. In a large pan, heat oil over medium heat. Add onions, garlic, and ginger, cooking until softened.
2. Add curry powder, turmeric, and cumin, cooking for 1 minute to release the flavors.
3. Add chicken or lamb and cook until browned. Stir in yogurt, cream, almonds, and chicken broth. Simmer for 20 minutes.
4. Season with salt to taste and garnish with cilantro. Serve with rice.

Goulash

Ingredients:

- 1 lb beef stew meat, cubed
- 2 tablespoons vegetable oil
- 1 onion, chopped
- 2 cloves garlic, minced
- 2 tablespoons paprika
- 1/2 teaspoon ground caraway seeds
- 1 bell pepper, chopped
- 1 can diced tomatoes (14.5 oz)
- 4 cups beef broth
- Salt and pepper to taste
- Cooked egg noodles, for serving

Instructions:

1. In a large pot, heat vegetable oil over medium heat. Brown beef in batches, then remove and set aside.
2. In the same pot, sauté onion, garlic, and bell pepper until softened.
3. Stir in paprika, caraway seeds, and diced tomatoes. Add beef back into the pot, along with beef broth.
4. Simmer for 1-1.5 hours until the beef is tender. Season with salt and pepper.
5. Serve over cooked egg noodles.

Pork Schnitzel

Ingredients:

- 4 boneless pork chops, pounded thin
- 1/2 cup all-purpose flour
- 2 large eggs, beaten
- 1 cup breadcrumbs
- 1 teaspoon salt
- 1/2 teaspoon pepper
- Vegetable oil, for frying
- Lemon wedges, for serving

Instructions:

1. Dredge each pork chop in flour, dip into beaten eggs, and coat with breadcrumbs.
2. Heat vegetable oil in a skillet over medium-high heat. Fry the schnitzels for 3-4 minutes per side, or until golden and cooked through.
3. Drain on paper towels and serve with lemon wedges.

www.ingramcontent.com/pod-product-compliance
Lightning Source LLC
LaVergne TN
LVHW081326060526
838201LV00055B/2486